MISS SPIDER'S WEDDING

paintings and verse by David Kirk

PUFFIN

A CALLAWAY EDITION

PUFFIN BOOKS

Published by the Penguin Group
Penguin Books Ltd, 80 Strand, London WC2R 0RL, England
Penguin Group (USA) Inc., 375 Hudson Street, New York, New York 10014, USA
Penguin Group (Canada), 90 Eglinton Avenue East, Suite 700, Toronto, Ontario, Canada M4P 2Y3 (a division of Pearson Penguin Canada Inc.)
Penguin Ireland, 25 St Stephen's Green, Dublin 2, Ireland (a division of Penguin Books Ltd)
Penguin Group (Australia), 250 Camberwell Road, Camberwell, Victoria 3124, Australia (a division of Pearson Australia Group Pty Ltd)
Penguin Books India Pvt Ltd, 11 Community Centre, Panchsheel Park, New Delhi – 110 017, India
Penguin Group (NZ), cnr Airborne and Rosedale Roads, Albany, Auckland 1310, New Zealand (a division of Pearson New Zealand Ltd)
Penguin Books (South Africa) (Pty) Ltd, 24 Sturdee Avenue, Rosebank, Johannesburg 2196, South Africa

Penguin Books Ltd, Registered Offices: 80 Strand, London WC2R 0RL, England

www.penguin.com

First published in the USA by Scholastic Press, in association with Callaway & Kirk Company LLC 1995
First published in Great Britain in Puffin Books 2006
1 3 5 7 9 10 8 6 4 2

Copyright © 1995 by Callaway & Kirk Company LLC. All rights reserved.

The moral right of the author and illustrator has been asserted
Miss Spider and all related characters are trademarks and/or registered trademarks of Callaway & Kirk Company LLC.

Set in AlKoch Antigua
Made and printed in China by South China Printing Company Co. Ltd

British Library Cataloguing in Publication Data
A CIP catalogue record for this book is available from the British Library

ISBN-13: 978-0-141-50072-0
ISBN-10: 0-141-50072-7

The paintings in this book are oils on paper.

Perhaps perfection seems too bold
A word here to apply.
For once love penetrates the heart,
It spreads to cloud the eye.

Still we in blindness take a chance
And gladly join in Cupid's dance.
For every joyful heart has shown,
Perfection dwells in love alone.

"Good morning, Miss! A lovely day."
Miss Spider spun around
To see Ike hanging by his knees
Three inches from the ground.

"My good friend Holley," Ike went on,
"Is someone you should know.
But he's too timid to come down
Or even say hello."

They heard a snap and then a crash
And gasped as Holley tumbled.
He flopped down at Miss Spider's feet,
Embarrassed, stunned and rumpled.

Miss Spider knelt to help him up.
He blushed, too shy to speak.
She bid demurely, "Won't you come
To tea one day this week?"

The colour drained from Holley's face.
He looked as though he'd swoon.
His acorn hat slipped from his head.
He gulped, "This afternoon?"

And when she heard his little voice,
It seemed to her somehow
That she had known him always
Though they'd never met 'til now . . .

"Please pay attention when I speak.
Stop daydreaming!" barked May.
Miss Spider's thoughts were still upon
The man she'd met that day.

May nagged, "You should get on with life.
I thought by now you'd be a wife!"
"But I –" Miss Spider tried to say.
"You mustn't interrupt!" sniffed May.

May jabbered on and on and on . . .
Miss Spider, with her patience gone,
Surveyed the clock and tapped the floor,
But when a face peeked round the door,

She whispered, "I apologize,
But, May, I just now realize,
A gentleman who asked to call
Is waiting for me in the hall."

"A man?" squealed May. "Well, finally!"
She dashed right out so she could see,
Then screamed, "Get lost, you puny pest.
She's waiting for her special guest!"

Miss Spider scurried towards the din.
She took his hand, then led him in.
May cried, "How can I stop her folly?
She's desperate if she's dating Holley!"

They talked of all their dreams and hopes,
Of art and nature, love and fate.
They peered through toy kaleidoscopes
And murmured thoughts I shan't relate.

Then Holley held Miss Spider's hand . . .
I'll say no more, you understand.
For private moments between spiders
Should not be witnessed by outsiders.

Back home, May snipped at Ike, her mate,
"Miss Spider's come undone!
That milksop Holley is her date.
Go fetch a better one!

"Be certain he's intelligent,
Strong, handsome, brave and elegant.
Just find an eight-legged Mr Right
And bring him back here by tonight."

Ike said, "But I think Holley
Is particularly nice.
It's not just me who thinks so.
You can go and ask the mice.

"They say he's helpful, wise and kind
And always so polite.
Perhaps he's just the one to be
Miss Spider's Mr Right."

May gasped, "You've lost your senses too!
That sissy bug will never do.
What difference if he's kind and wise?
He isn't half Miss Spider's size.

"I see I'll have to go with you.
For very clearly, Ike,
You simply do not have a clue
To what we women like."

"This fellow here, for instance,
Is no proper type at all.
He's drunk so much petunia wine,
He's hardly fit to crawl.

"His web is coarse and slovenly,
With clothes strewn all about.
I could not see Miss Spider wed
To that disgraceful lout!

"I'm certain even you can see
These spiders will not suit.
The green one is a crybaby;
The white one is a brute!

"Our gentle friend could not endure
The likes of either one, I'm sure.
How could she hope to overcome
Their temperaments so quarrelsome?

"Now there's a really handsome hunk
Of spider specimen.
A bevy of admirers wait
To fawn all over him.

"His web is tidy and well made,
His shoes all in a row.
The length of nose to eyebrow is
The perfect ratio."

May called, "Oh, spider sir, yoo-hoo!
I've got the perfect girl for you."
She whispered, "Now I'll put things right."
"I hope," squeaked Ike, "he doesn't bite."

"Please tell me of this lonely miss,"
The spider strongman cooed.
"Is she a beauty? Is she rich?
And is she in the mood . . .

"To be adroitly charmed and wooed
By dashing, handsome me?
But how could it be otherwise!"
He laughed triumphantly.

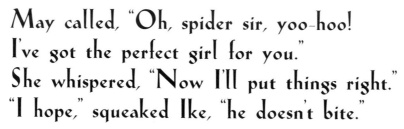

"Why don't you beetle darlings
Wait right here 'til I come back.
You'll be – I mean, I'll make for you
A tasty little snack.

"You'll find it cosy on my web.
The view is fine from here.
So rest your tired abdomens
Until I reappear."

Miss Spider later welcomed in
This strange arachnid gentleman.
His air was fine, his manner grand.
He bowed and kissed her dainty hand.

"I've journeyed here, dear lady,
From the Land of Falling Leaves.
Please let me introduce myself,
I'm called Spiderus Reeves.

"Fair princess, to that distant place
Flowed stories of your charm and grace.
But none of them, I must confess,
Prepared me for your loveliness."

"My darling, I can plainly see
That you are everything to me.
I long to know the soul within
Your lovely exoskeleton.

He peered around the drawing room
At all the finery.
He coveted the furnishings,
The carpets and settee.

"Is it mere chance? No, it is fate,
That soon we shall co-webitate.
'Twas set down by a will divine
That I am yours and you are mine.

All this, he thought, would soon be mine
If she and I were wed.
He mused, Her house will suit me well.
But here is what he said:

"My angel, let us not delay,"
The sly Spiderus said.
"Tomorrow is the perfect day
For you and I to wed."

"Kind sir, you move too fast for me,"
Miss Spider cried protestingly.
"My love already has been spun
And promised to another one."

"You cannot mean," Spiderus howled,
"That you're rejecting me!
Tell me this loathsome rival's name;
I'll squash him like a flea!"

His hot breath sprayed Miss Spider's face –
With all the force he had,
He screamed, "You will reveal his name!"
She said, "I won't, you cad!"

He turned his back and brayed, "I must
Go find and grind him into dust!
So, foolish woman, be forewarned,
Spiderus Reeves shall not be scorned."

At that same moment in the hall,
Poor Holley, staring at the wall,
Could dwell on one and just one thought,
Does she love me? Does she not?

He could not sleep, although he tried.
His weary brain was occupied,
Envisioning her fine assets,
Her gentle curves, her spinnerets.

Those emerald eyes, so deep, so green,
Like nothing he had ever seen.
Her sweet round face, that pointed nose!
And lips to shame the red, red rose.

He tossed and tumbled in his web,
Recalling every word she'd said,
Then paced the garden in the gloom
As shadows swept across the moon.

Just then there was a little sound
That didn't seem quite right.
He cocked his head and heard two voices
Whimpering in fright.

He rushed to find poor Ike and May,
And ripped their sticky bonds away,
But turned when someone in mid-air
Roared, "Speck! What are you doing there?"

"I'm merely snipping a few strands,
Kind sir, because you see,
You've caught this beetle couple
In your web mistakenly.

"It's only luck that brings me here
Down from my web above.
I'd be asleep but for the thought
Of dear Miss Spider's love."

"And so it's you," Spiderus snarled,
"Who dares to interfere.
There's been just one mistake, my friend,
But I shall fix it here.

"You've freed those tasty beetles
I was going to eat in bed.
That's just too bad, for now I'm forced
To eat you up instead!"

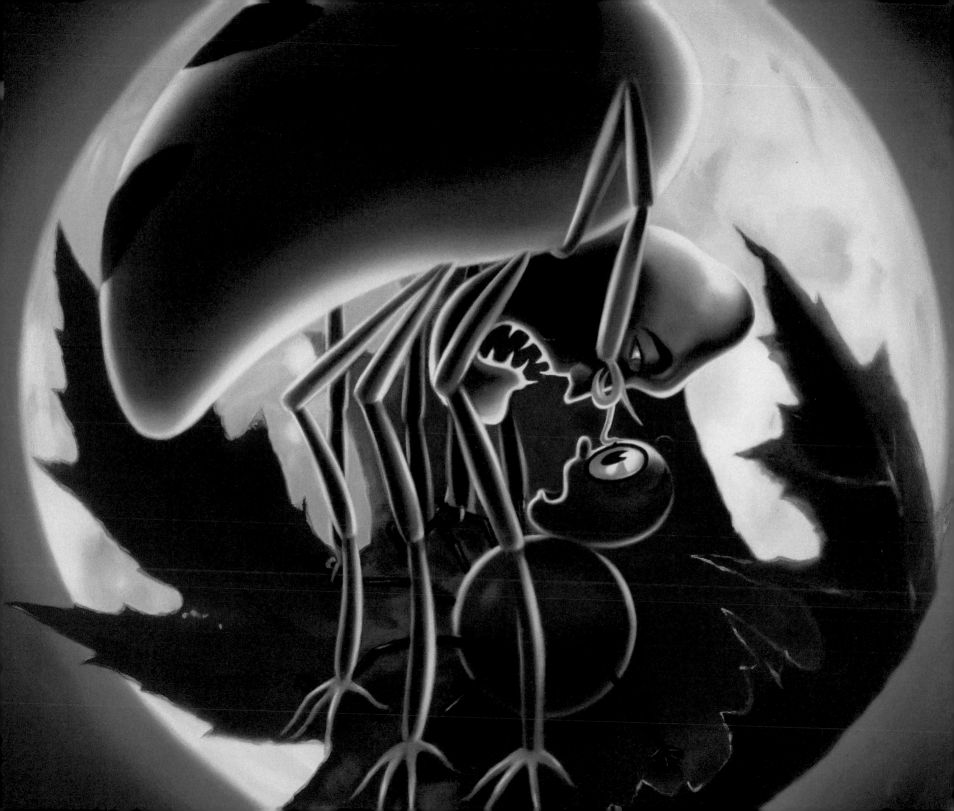

Holley's life flashed before his eyes
Peering up that toothy jaw.
As everything was growing dim,
Fading out, he thought he saw

An angel swoop down in a gown
Of yellow flecked with black,
Who shrieked, "Let go of him, you brute!"
And smacked the scoundrel's back.

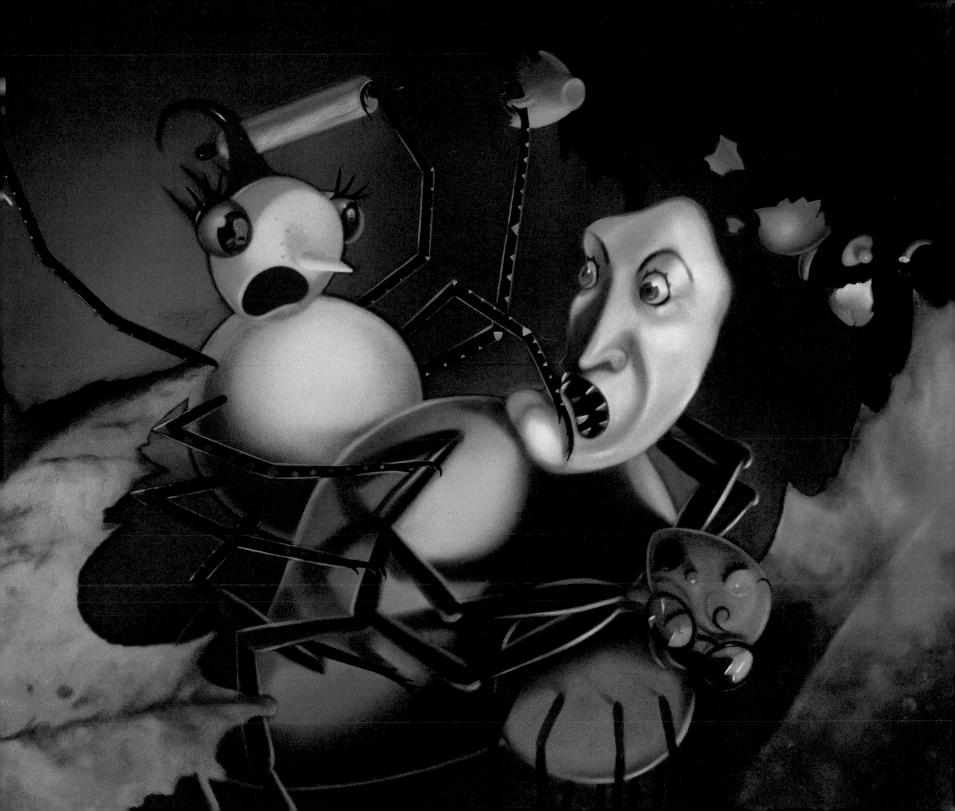

Drifting back to consciousness,
Holley sensed someone he knew . . .
Yes, yes, Miss Spider's lovely face
Came swimming into view.

"Darling, are you back with me?"
His spider nurse begged hopefully.
"I've tried a hundred different ways
To wake you up for three whole days!"

He gazed upon her reverently,
Then wobbling to her side,
Looked up into her eyes and whispered,
"Will you be my bride?"

A blush of scarlet tinged her cheek.
Her lips, aquiver, could not speak.
He stroked her gently with his feet.
She murmured softly, "Yes, my sweet."

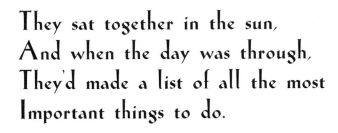

They sat together in the sun,
And when the day was through,
They'd made a list of all the most
Important things to do.

The crickets would be asked to play
The music on their wedding day.
The field mice, woolly bears and bees
Would cater an affair to please!

"I'll bake the cake," Miss Spider said,
"And weave my silken veils."
Then Holley peeped, "I'll spin a suit
With silk top hat and tails!

"We'll send an invitation out
To every bug alive,
With notices in every bush
And treetop, hill and hive."

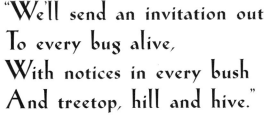

"Can any have the slightest doubt?"
Chirps Holley with a smile,

"The fairest creature in the world
Is walking down the aisle,

"To be my own beloved bride,
My joy and comfort, hope and pride!

"I feel my life has just begun!
Now she and I will be as one."

"Oh see how handsome Holley looks!"
Miss Spider sings with glee.
"Of all the spiders in the world,
He chose to be with me.
We've found the place where love abides,
And share the warmth that it provides
For all those who have found the way
To savour life's most sweet bouquet."

The butterflies swirl high above
To view this scene of spider love
And promise of eternal bliss,
As Holley and Miss Spider kiss.

The banquet table's loaded high
With treats like crispy aphid pie,
Grilled dandelions and bug-eyed peas,
Sweet pickled grapes and mouse-milk cheese.

With crickets fiddling in full swing,
The katydids begin to sing.
June beetles spin in pirouettes,
As clickbugs clack like castanets.

The drinks are served by Honey Bee.
Petunia wine is flowing free.
The guests are eager to give kisses
To dear Miss Spider, now a "Mrs".

The bride and groom, at last withdrawn
From all the chaos on the lawn,
Poise low upon a willow tree
And hold each other tenderly.

We see their forms in silhouette;
Their shapes are clear to us, and yet,
How can we fully recognize
The beauty seen through true love's eyes?